arabia

AT THE TIME OF MOHAMMED SHOWING TRADE AND CARAVAN ROUTES AND NOMADIC TRIBES (UNDERLINED)

PERSIA (IRAN)

GULF

SEA ROUTES FROM INDIA

IPTY QUARTER
(SAND)

MAUT

ARABIAN SEA

SEA ROUTE FROM INDIA

RAIN FROM INDIAN OCEAN

mohammed

لـبـ ويو وهمـ
لـ.حو ذ هم
ا لله. لا حمـ

ISBN 0 00 192245 9
First Published 1972
© Text and illustrations Bernard Brett 1972
Printed in Great Britain by William Collins Sons & Co. Ltd., Glasgow

mohammed

BERNARD BRETT

COLLINS

Arabia and its People

The story of Mohammed began in Arabia, a large peninsula lying between the Persian Gulf in the east and the Red Sea in the west, with the Arabian Sea to the south. Mountain ranges run down the whole of the west and along much of the south coasts, allowing very little of the rain from these two directions to reach the interior, which is desert or semi-desert. The country is bleak and uninviting, the sun scorches the vast gravel beds and stretches of shimmering sand, thinly covered with thorny bushes and scrub. Here and there, bare mountains of rock jut suddenly out of the flat wilderness.

Scattered throughout this desert region are occasional springs and wells, permanent oases where date palms flourish, wheat, barley and maize grow, and domestic animals graze. In the sixth century A.D. this barren land was the home of wandering tribes of nomads. At this time there were two types of Arab; the oasis- or town-dweller, who settled for generations in the one spot; and the nomad or wanderer.

The nomads were natural fighters and pioneers, and it was they who became the staunchest supporters of Mohammed. These hardy tribes of desert people lived in black tents woven by the women from goat's hair. They ate very little, existing on a handful of dates, bread, a

porridge made from flour, and rice. Only on very rare occasions did they eat meat, as the animals were needed to trade for their other food. Their camels, sheep and goats did supply them with milk, butter and cheese, and they also drank the often bitter water from the rank desert water holes. Their life was a hard one, for even in good years the grazing only lasted a few days, and scouts had always to be sent ahead to seek out fresh pastures. When they returned, the tents would be quickly taken down and packed together with the nomads' few possessions on the backs of the baggage camels. Then the whole tribe would move off, straggling across the desert to their next pasture, the women and children following, their shouts mingling with the bleating of sheep and goats which they drove ahead of them.

Although they usually kept to their own recognized areas, in bad seasons the search for grass often caused them to travel hundreds of miles, sometimes taking them into country occupied by other tribes. This led to tribal wars which they accepted as part of the normal way of life. The fighting, though fierce while it lasted, left no deep hatred

6

between the tribes; they fought only to survive, raiding their neighbours' flocks or attempting to drive them from water holes and grazing areas. They also fought to a strict code of honour, and treachery was considered shameful. Usually when tribes went to war with each other, they agreed weeks or even months ahead on a time and place to do battle.

Very few nomads could read or write, but many were natural poets; their verses and sagas were handed down from generation to generation. They were also a generous people; no traveller was ever turned away from their tents, and they would kill their last sheep to supply a feast for a guest.

Strangers would arrive to be greeted by hordes of dogs and children; their host would lead them to his tent and seat them on the tribal rugs. As they drank goat's milk, the guests would be shown the household pets: the watch cockerel, the hawk, the hunting greyhound. Then the food would be carried in, steaming on a large copper tray; white rice swimming in liquid butter, covered with legs and ribs of mutton, with a boiled sheep's head carefully placed in the centre. Everyone then set to: rolling up their sleeves to the elbow, they dipped their hands into the rice and meat, rolling the greasy food into neat balls before slipping it into their mouths, the right hand only being used for eating. The chief guest would be given the sheep's eyeballs as a special treat. At last, full to bursting, the travellers would sit back, having eaten more food than the whole tribe would consume in a week. There were no written laws, but the old and weak were protected by the rest of the tribe as a matter of course. Blood feuds were practised, which had to be avenged at all costs. The Arabs say, "The man of men is he who thinks early and late how he can injure his enemies and do his friends good."

The majority of Arabs were nomads, but some settled permanently at oases in the interior, sometimes building towns and cities. These were farmers and merchants: careful, hardworking people who rarely took part in tribal wars and raids. Though generous, they did not provide the princely banquets of the nomads. But they too indulged in blood feuds. Lesser merchants from these oases travelled among the nomads, trading their rugs, dates, rice and copper pans, for wool, butter and livestock. The more important merchants travelled in caravans from oasis to oasis, even crossing the dangerous, unfriendly deserts that lay between them and the rich countries of Syria, Persia and Egypt, bringing back with them not only the produce of these countries, but ideas, which they introduced into their own cities. Gradually the Arab towns and cities began to absorb these civilizing influences, and by the sixth century they were skilled in mathematics, astronomy, science and medicine. Yet the fiercely independent desert people tended to despise these city dwellers, whom they regarded as their inferiors.

Mecca

Hidden in a savage valley, surrounded by barren rocky mountains lies Mecca, the Holy City of the Arabs. In the sixth century it was one of the few watering places on the wealthy Oriental caravan routes, lying midway between Syria and the Yemen on the eastern shore of the Red Sea. This made it an important trading centre; every caravan travelling either north or south stopped there to refill their water skins, buy food and barter for local wares. It was also important because it was the centre of idol worship, to which the nomadic tribes of Arabia made annual pilgrimage.

The Book of Genesis tells how when Hagar was expelled from the tents of Abraham with her baby son Ishmael, she wandered over the desert until she reached the stony valley of Mecca. Her food had given out, her water gourd was empty and, nearly dead from thirst, she laid her baby under a thorny acacia, covered her head with her cloak and prepared to die. Suddenly an angel appeared and led her to a well, so

that both she and Ishmael were saved. The early Arabs called the well Zem-Zem because of the bubbling noise it made.

The Bible claims that it was one of the oldest wells in the world, the Arabs say it goes right back to Adam. It was on this spot that Abraham and Ishmael founded the settlement that was to become the city of Mecca. Built in the midst of black unfriendly hills and glaring desert, with little shade from the fiery rays of the sun and its only vegetation thorny acacias, Mecca was an uninviting place. By the sixth century it had grown from a collection of mud huts into a large important city. Its houses, tall, flat-roofed buildings made of the local grey stone, clung precariously to the hillside. Latticed balconies overhung the crowded streets, which were narrow and winding, noisy with the shouts of merchants and traders, and always dusty. Camels, heavily laden with silks, spices and wine from the North, padded majestically through the

dust, jostling stubborn pack mules and donkeys, as they were driven on with sticks by their masters. The shops and eating places were loud with the clamour of different tongues; Syrian, Persian, and Egyptian, mingled with Arabic dialects from every part of the peninsula; caravan owners haggled and gossiped over cups of thick, sweet coffee.

The people of Mecca were very proud of their city, and considered themselves to be the most cultured people in Arabia, speaking the purest Arabic.

In the centre of the town close to the Zem-Zem well stood the Kaaba, the holy shrine of the Arab world. Made of grey stone and standing forty feet high, it was a cube-shaped roofless building without windows. Crude statues of gods were brought to Mecca from every part of Arabia, Syria and as far afield as Egypt. By the sixth century there were 360 roughly-hewn idols crammed together inside the building, each representing a separate god or goddess. Outside, sunk into the corner of one of the walls was the Black Stone. The Arabs believed that the

stone came from Paradise and had been given to Abraham and Ishmael by the angel Gabriel. Once snow white, it had become black through being kissed by the millions of sinners who made the pilgrimage to Mecca. Legend had it that Adam built the first Kaaba, to represent the single God of the Jews, but with time it became the custom of the other tribes who believed in more than one God, to make an annual pilgrimage to the sacred place.

The Lord of the Kaaba was Allah. "Allah" is not a name, but comes from the Arabic "Alilah" meaning "the God". Other idols in the Kaaba represented Hubal, a mighty image carved from a single block of agate, Abraham and Ishmael, and Jesus and the Virgin Mary.

It was to worship these gods that Arabs came from every part of the peninsula. A powerful group of clans called the Quraish were the most important tribe in Mecca, and their leaders ruled the city. They were merchants who organized the annual pilgrimage to Mecca which lasted three days, providing food and shelter for the pilgrims in return for which they were paid a tax called Rifada. As well as this the Quraish also had religious duties.

Mohammed was born in Mecca about 570 years after the birth of Christ. His father had married Amina of the Beni Zuhra clan of the Quraish, but he died before his son was born. The baby's grandfather, Abdul Muttalib, a famous warrior and a guardian of the Quraish, named the child, Mohammed, "the Praised".

Although his grandfather was rich and powerful, because of his father's death Mohammed and his mother remained poor. It was the custom to send children of the wealthy citizens to be nursed by the desert tribes, in order to avoid the stifling, unhealthy heat of Mecca, but because of their poverty Mohammed's mother had great difficulty in finding anyone to take her child. Eventually Haleema, a woman of the Beni Saad tribe agreed to look after him, and Mohammed remained among the black tents of his foster parents until he was six years old, often going with the other children to mind the flocks of sheep. Later he used to say, "There is no prophet but has worked as a shepherd. I herded sheep as a boy."

Soon after his return to the Holy City his mother died and Mohammed went to live with his grandfather; but two years later he also died, so the young boy was finally adopted by his uncle, Abu Talib, a wealthy merchant. Arab historians say, that when he was twelve years old Mohammed begged his uncle to take him on a caravan journey to Syria. There at a town called Bosra a Christian monk foretold that one day he would become a prophet. From then on Mohammed accompanied Abu Talib on all his trading missions. By the age of sixteen he had travelled further than most Meccans travelled in a lifetime.

Mohammed with the shepherds

As he grew older Mohammed began to gain a reputation not only for

his success as a caravan merchant, but for his honesty, his nickname in Mecca being "The Trustworthy". It was during his travels that he first began to question the idol worship of the Kaaba. On his journeys to Syria, Persia and Palestine, he met men of many different religions, particularly Christians, Jews and Zoroastrians (Fire worshippers). Discussing religion with them he was impressed by their belief in a single god who had created the universe, and governed the lives of men. The teaching of Jesus Christ and the Jewish prophets caused him to question his own gods, and much of what they taught made sense to him. He began to doubt the power of the stone idols of the Kaaba, and wonder if it were wrong to worship them. However it was difficult for him to throw over the teaching of his childhood and he was worried by his doubts.

For two years Mohammed managed the caravans of a rich and influential widow in Mecca, named Khadija, travelling on her behalf as far afield as Damascus, Aleppo, Jerusalem, Antioch and Baalbek. Khadija became very fond of Mohammed and eventually they married in 595 when Mohammed was 25 and Khadija was 40.

Merchants of Mecca

The Call

After his marriage Mohammed continued to help Khadija in her business, but little is known of this period of his life. When he was 35 years old, it was decided that the Kaaba should be rebuilt. Rain had washed away the foundations and it was considered to be unsafe. All went well until the walls were high enough to replace the Black Stone, when each clan of the Quraish claimed the right to place the stone in position. This led to violent quarrels which seemed likely to end in bloodshed. The oldest member of the Quraish persuaded the others to leave the decision to the first person to enter the courtyard in which the Kaaba stood. This turned out to be Mohammed. When the problem was explained to him, he spread a cloak on the ground on which he laid the Black Stone. He then ordered the leaders of each clan to take hold of the edge of the cloak and lift it to the required height, and Mohammed himself placed the stone in its niche before another quarrel could break out. This simple solution considerably increased Mohammed's reputation among the elders of the Quraish. About this time Mohammed adopted two young men as his sons, two sons of his own having died as infants. One was Ali, son of his uncle Abu Talib, the other was Zaid, a Syrian, whom Khadija had given him as a personal slave, and these were to remain his most devoted followers throughout his life.

Gradually Mohammed began to take less and less interest in his wife's business and spend more of his time thinking about religion, and the

The angel Gabriel appears to Mohammed

ideas of the people he had met on his travels. He was finding it increasingly difficult to accept the idols of the Kaaba as being anything more than lifeless blocks of granite and stone. His belief in the Christian and Jewish idea of a single god grew stronger as his faith in the Kaaba became less. A few miles outside Mecca, isolated in the desert stood Mount Hira, a huge rock, polished smooth by sand and wind, which made an ideal place for quiet meditation. It was there in a small cave that Mohammed would go to get away from the noisy alleys of Mecca. He began to spend most of his time there. He would often sit for days puzzled by the confusing thoughts running through his head. He was becoming con-

20

vinced in his own mind that there could only be one god, not just for Christians and Jews but for the whole of mankind. But he still felt uneasy about throwing over a lifetime's belief in the Kaaba.

As he had always eaten well and was used to an active life in the open air, his new way of life began to affect his health. He rarely slept, and when he did he was troubled by strange, disturbing dreams; and often he had fainting fits or went into convulsions. Although she was worried, Khadija tried to do everything she could to help her husband during this difficult time. She is credited with saying that Mohammed would suddenly begin to tremble violently and faint away, perspiring heavily even in the coldest weather. Then he would lie for long periods, eyes tightly closed, moaning. Some years later during the month of Ramadan, when Arabs fast between sunrise and sunset for thirty days, Mohammed went as usual to his cave on Mount Hira to meditate and pray. According to Arab legend, as Mohammed lay on the floor of the cave, he heard a loud clear voice call to him twice. Thinking it was a djinn or evil spirit, he fainted with fear. When he recovered consciousness, as he later related to his followers, he saw the dazzling figure of the angel Gabriel, standing before him.

"Read thou," commanded Gabriel.

"I cannot," replied Mohammed.

"Read thou, in the name of the Lord who created all things from earth; read in the name of the Most High, who taught man the use of the pen, and taught him what before he knew not."

Recalling this experience later, Mohammed told how he rushed from the cave in terror, intending to throw himself off the mountain top, but halfway up a voice from heaven called, "O Mohammed, Thou art the Messenger of God". It was then that he knew that he must spread the idea of a single god. He told only Khadija and his two adopted sons about his vision, and because of their faith in him, they came to believe in his idea of a single god for all men. But because of the jealousy of the powerful leaders of the Kaaba, he had to move cautiously, and during the first two years of his mission he made only forty converts. Then came the turning point: Gabriel once again appeared to him on Mount Hira and this time commanded him to go out and preach to the world.

Mohammed preaching

The Persecution

Mohammed first called a meeting of the Quraish in the desert, where he
preached that Allah was the only god. As no one took any notice, he
next held a dinner for the elders of his family, and announced himself to
them as the Messenger of God. Led by his uncle, Abu Lahab, they
laughed at his ideas and made fun of him. Opinion in Mecca was that he
was possessed by a djinn, and he was treated either with sympathy or
ridicule, but at this stage there was little opposition to him, as most
Meccans did not take him seriously. But this man with his obvious sin-
cerity, and white hot, passionate beliefs, began to win over many followers to his cause. However, when he attacked the gods of the Kaaba,
calling them senseless blocks of stone, the majority of Meccans became
very angry. His bitterest enemy was one of the most respected men in the
city, Abu Jahal, and he accused Mohammed of using magical powers to
split families and set father against son. Now the people began to sneer
openly at Mohammed and these sneers turned to violence; he and

his followers were stoned and beaten, and many went in fear of their lives. Mohammed was forced to send some of his disciples to Abyssinia for safety, where they were welcomed by the King, a Christian who was tolerant of the new religion. Only the protection of his powerful uncle, Abu Talib, saved Mohammed himself from being murdered. The ideas that Mohammed preached had much in common with the Christian and Jewish religions, and though he disagreed with many of their teachings, particularly the Christian "Trinity", he believed they all had the same one god. Mohammed was firmly convinced that he was the Messenger of Allah, the god of Islam, as the new religion came to be called. So throughout his life he related his revelations and messages to his followers, who wrote them down on any odd scraps of material: oyster shells, shoulder bones of sheep, bits of wood, strips of leather, anything that happened to be at hand at the time. These were kept safely in a box, and after Mohammed's death they were put together to form the 114 chapters of the Koran, the holy book of Islam. Although Mohammed preached against the idols of the Kaaba, he believed that Allah, Lord of the Kaaba, was the unseen, supreme being who had

The stoning of Mohammed and his followers

created mankind and the universe. He told of a paradise after death, where the poorest camel driver could live forever in luxury. This strongly appealed to the desert nomads, whose lives were spent in a miserable attempt to keep alive. Mohammed gave his followers a creed and five obligatory duties.

They should believe in no god but Allah.

They should believe in God's angels.

They should believe in His books, all of which had been lost except the Book of Moses, David's Psalms, the Gospel of Jesus, and Mohammed's Koran.

They should believe in His prophets, the greatest of these being Adam, Noah, Moses, Jesus and Mohammed.

They should believe in the Resurrection and the Day of Judgement.

They should believe that everything that has ever happened or will ever happen, was and will be the will of Allah.

Their duties were to recite the creed five times a day, fast during Ramadan, for those that could afford it, pilgrimage to Mecca and, lastly, give alms to the community and the destitute.

He also forbade the eating of pork as unclean, and the drinking of alcohol as ungodly.

The Flight

Mohammed in hiding

In 619 Khadija died. Mohammed was grief-stricken. Abu Talib also died in the same year. With his last protector gone, Mohammed's enemies became more confident. They threatened his life, and many of his followers fled to Medina for safety.

Medina lay two hundred miles from Mecca, a large oasis of date palms and flowers, surrounded by steep cliffs and sandy desert. Three important tribes of Jews lived in Medina, and though powerful, they were ruled by two Arab tribes, the Beni Aus and the Beni Khazraj. Some members of the Khazraj heard Mohammed preaching at a fair outside Mecca, and believed him to be the Messiah the Jews of Medina had been expecting for centuries. Now here he was, not a Jew but an Arab, one of them. They hurried back to Medina and told the city leaders, who later met Mohammed in the desert outside Mecca, and swore to serve him. Their oath was, We will obey the Prophet in everything that is right, and will be faithful to him in wealth and in sorrow.

To help bind his followers to him, Mohammed arranged a number of marriages. He himself took two wives, Aisha daughter of his friend Abu Bekr, and Sawda, the widow of another friend. His own three daughters married three of his most powerful allies.

Despite the fierce hatred of the guardians of the Kaaba, Mohammed

30

remained in Mecca for a further three years. Then Abu Jahal planned his murder. A member of each clan of the Quraish was to plunge a sword into the body of Mohammed, so that no single clan should be blamed. Late that night they hurried silently through the black, deserted streets to Mohammed's house, but he had been warned of the plot and had already fled with a friend into the desert, where he hid for three days in a cave.

When it was discovered that Mohammed had escaped, Abu Jahal offered a reward of a hundred camels for his capture. The men of Mecca began to scour the desert for him. Once a group of horsemen of the Quraish stopped outside his hiding place, but a spider had spun its web right across the mouth of the cave and the soldiers did not think it worth while to search inside. Mohammed's friend, Abu Bekr, was terrified, but the Prophet told him, "Mourn not, for Allah is surely with us."

On the third night, a nomad who knew that part of the desert brought two fast camels to the cave. Under the light of a crescent moon the three men set out on the dangerous journey to Medina, avoiding the usual caravan routes. The way lay over beds of lava rock, endless sand dunes, and stretches of burning gravel; nothing grew, nothing lived in this wilderness.

Setting out from Damascus

The Battle of Bedr

A week later Mohammed and his companions arrived at Kuba, an oasis near Medina. Here they were met by many sympathisers, who escorted them into Medina. Thousands of citizens turned out to welcome their Prophet, who allowed his camel to pick its own way through the winding streets and groves of date palms. Eventually it stopped and knelt in an open space shaded by clumps of tall trees, and here Mohammed vowed to build his first place of worship. Within twenty-four hours the ground had been cleared and the foundations begun. Mohammed and his followers had little money or food; they had been insulted and persecuted for years by the Quraish, and they now decided to hit back at their enemies. The fact that they could not work at their trades and professions in Medina increased their poverty, and new means of survival had to be found.

Mohammed began to send out parties to waylay Meccan caravans travelling to Syria, but only once did they succeed in capturing one. This was a small caravan carrying dried raisins, skins and wine, which was attacked during a holy period of truce. The Meccan merchants were naturally against fighting, as it interfered with trade, but they were so angry at the breaking of a truce, that they decided to take up arms against Mohammed at the first opportunity.

Every year a great caravan was sent from Mecca to trade in Syria. That autumn the annual caravan set out from Damascus on its return journey to Mecca: a thousand camels heavily laden with riches of the north, representing a large part of the yearly income of the Holy City. Mohammed's spies rode night and day to bring him the news that the caravan was on its way home. Mohammed immediately set out from Medina with 314 men to capture this wealthy prize; but they had only seventy camels and two horses between them. Taking it in turn to ride, they somehow

covered the eighty miles of rocky desert to the wells of Bedr, where they hoped to surprise the caravan. However, Abu Jahal, learning of Mohammed's intention, sent his best riders on their racing camels to warn the caravan to take another route. Then, gathering together a Quraish war party of a thousand well-armed men mounted on camels and horses, he rushed headlong from the city to do battle with Mohammed.

The two armies met in the Bedr valley. The battle began according to Arab rules and custom, with the two sides facing each other out of arrow range; then three champions of the Quraish rode forward, insulting Mohammed's followers and challenging them to single combat. Three of Mohammed's relatives took up the challenge and killed all three Meccan warriors. This was the sign for general combat. As Mohammed charged at the head of his followers, two black flags streaming behind him, a sudden squall of wind blew sand into the faces of the Meccans. "Gabriel," shouted the Prophet, "with a thousand angels is falling upon the enemy." Confused, the Meccans wavered, then broke completely and fled back to their city, leaving seventy dead, including their leader Abu Jahal. This was the first military victory for Islam. After this victory converts began to flock to Mohammed's banner, and despite being defeated and himself wounded at the battle of Uhud, he and his followers were becoming a powerful force in Arabia. The Quraish decided the only way to stop Mohammed was to drive him from Medina. Gathering an army of 10,000 men they rode against the city.

Mohammed, warned of the approaching army, looked at his own warriors, barely 3,000 in all, many of them badly armed and untrained. He realized the Meccans would attack from the south, where the streets of Medina ran into the gardens and palm groves, and were undefended. The houses on the other sides of the city formed a strong, impregnable rampart, and a wall of high cliffs guarded the northern end. The attack had to come from the south, but how to defend it with only 3,000 men? Then one of Mohammed's followers, a Persian, Salem, came to him with an idea. He had seen ditches too wide for a horse to jump used in siege warfare. Would it be possible to dig such a ditch in time? The Prophet himself, stripped to the waist, led the digging; by working day and night it was at last finished. When the splendidly armed and mounted Meccan cavalry finally reached the city, they found themselves faced with a deep trench, defended by 3,000 resolute warriors, firing arrows from behind banks of earth. After a few half-hearted attempts to take the trench had

35

failed, they gave up the siege and returned to Mecca, discouraged and bedraggled by the icy rain that had begun to fall.

As Mohammed became stronger he sent envoys to the surrounding countries of Syria, Byzantium and Persia, where they were treated with courtesy and sent back with gifts.

At the time of the annual pilgrimage, Mohammed led 1,500 of his white-robed followers to Mecca. Here he signed a treaty with the Quraish, halting hostilities between the two cities. But two years later a

clan of the Quraish attacked a tribe paying allegiance to Mohammed. This gave him the excuse he had been waiting for.

Mohammed's army had now changed from an irregular, badly armed band of desert skirmishers into a highly disciplined force of 10,000 well-armed troops, officered by men experienced in warfare. On New Year's Day, Mohammed led his army from Medina. Great dust clouds rose as squadron after squadron of cavalry cantered over the parched earth towards Mecca. Meanwhile all roads to Mecca had been barred and the movements of all nomads stopped, so the attack came as a complete surprise to the city. Thrown into a panic the city elders of the Quraish surrendered and Mohammed's troops occupied Mecca. This was the Prophet's greatest triumph; he himself rode into the Holy City dressed in the simple white robes of a pilgrim, straight to the Kaaba, where he destroyed the 360 idols. Then he and his followers rode back to their homes in Medina. Mohammed's fame spread like a flame throughout Asia Minor. Delegates from all countries of the Near East now came to pay their respects to him. The King of Oman and the governor of Syria sent their representatives; the Yemen and Randramut embraced Islam. It seemed that this was the pinnacle of Mohammed's success, but still he was not satisfied, and impressed on his followers the vital need to carry Islam throughout the world. Although he was growing old Mohammed insisted on making one last pilgrimage to Mecca, the Holy City. The road from Medina had never seemed so long; when he arrived there he summoned his strength and preached to tens of thousands of his followers. ending by crying out, "O Lord! I have delivered my message and accomplished my work!" The multitude of pilgrims, as one, answered "Yea, verily thou hast."

Returning to Medina, Mohammed became ill with fever, his strength rapidly ebbed away and he died in June 632, aged 62. His last words were, "O Lord, pardon me and join me to the companionship on high. O Allah be it among all the glorious associates in Paradise."

Mohammed entering Mecca

Baghdad, the capital of Islam

The Expansion of Islam

The story of Islam did not end that June day when Mohammed died; in fact it was the beginning of the fulfilment of his ambitions for Islam. Within two hundred years his followers had conquered the greater part of the known world, creating one of the world's greatest empires, half as big again as the Roman Empire. Mohammed's friend Abu Bekr became his Successor, or Khalif, and immediately had to face a general rebellion of the Arab tribes who renounced Islam. During the following twelve months a series of bitter wars were fought, until finally all the tribes of Arabia once again accepted Islam. United again, the Muslims under Abu Bekr began their campaign to carry out Mohammed's wish to make Islam world-wide.

But it was not until Abu Bekr's death two years after that of Mohammed, and the succession of Omar as Khalif that the spread of Islam through conquest really began. The army of Islam was by now the largest and most powerful in the world; their battle cry, "Allah u Akbar!" (Allah is great) struck terror into their enemies. The cavalry under

41

Omar's generals, Khaled and Amr', swept like a tidal wave across Asia Minor. The hitherto invincible Roman Legions were defeated at Lake Tiberius, their eagles captured, and the whole of Syria subdued. Jerusalem, Aleppo, Antioch and Ceasares were taken, and the hordes of Islam surged into Mesopotamia and Persia. Egypt was invaded and conquered, the Persian army was destroyed and the Persian Empire ceased to exist. The Arabs reached the frontiers of China and occupied what is now West Pakistan. In the west they defeated the Visigoths. Advancing deep into France, they were finally stopped at Tours by the Franks in 732, less than three hundred miles from England. Throughout their conquests the Arabs always remembered the command of Mohammed to spread the word of Islam, which remained their main concern. Unlike previous conquerors, Huns, Goths and Mongols, they did not destroy cities and enslave the conquered: anyone embracing Islam was immediately accepted as an equal. They collected taxes but offered in return real protection, which they took very seriously. An Arab commander, forced out of Syria by a Roman army, returned all the taxes he had collected because he could no longer protect the Syrians.

732 saw the full extent of their conquests. Eighteen years later the Abbasids became the new rulers as the result of a revolt. They built the city of Baghdad, which they made the capital of Islam.

After this there were no more conquests: Islam was on the defensive and the empire began to grow smaller. The Abbasid rulers were more interested in commerce, science and culture than in conquest, and Baghdad became the wealthiest and most luxurious city in the world. Whilst Europe was still struggling in the "Dark Ages" Islam was advancing in every field of learning; and this learning was freely spread throughout the countries they occupied. Western Europe absorbed this learning, but their faith in Christianity was never shaken. Islam was a religion for people living a precarious life in the desert; the easier existence of the northern countries called for a less simple creed, with saints, priests and religious services. For Islam had neither saints nor priests; people were called to prayer at their mosques, morning and evening by the muezzin, and they prayed without any set services.

Medical schools flourished in Baghdad, where doctors had to take four years training and pass an examination before they were allowed to practise. Their text books on medicine, surgery and the treatment of eye complaints were so advanced that they remained the main works studied in European universities until the sixteenth century. During the Crusades the Arab surgeons were appalled at the crude methods of their Christian colleagues.

Arab astronomers were accurately measuring the circumference of the earth at a time when Europeans thought the world flat. They developed algebra, trigonometry and logarithms, and it was the Arabs who gave us our present numerals. The manufacture of paper was introduced into *Arab astronomers* Europe by the Muslims, along with rhyming verse.

The Franks stop the advance of Islam

Their command of the Mediterranean and the Indian Ocean gave them a tight hold on the world's commerce, and their merchant ships traded as far afield as China in the east and Britain in the west. Thus Mohammed's enthusiasm continued to grip the imagination of his followers, and they carried his teaching throughout the known world, which Islam dominated for 500 years following his death. He had welded the fierce, independent nomads of the desert and the farmers and merchants of the oases into one vital force, their centuries of squabbling and fighting put aside to carry out his will. This remains one of the miracles of history. Mohammed's teaching has continued to the present day. Islam has 430,000,000 followers throughout the world, and in size it is second only to Christianity.

45

Index